THE INSPIRATIONAL VIEW OF THE WORD OF GOD

THE INSPIRATIONAL VIEW OF THE WORD OF GOD

Kerry T. Lee

VANTAGE PRESS
New York

Cover design by Susan Thomas

FIRST EDITION

Copyright © 2004 by Kerry T. Lee

Published by Vantage Press, Inc.
419 Park Ave. South, New York, NY 10016

Manufactured in the United States of America
ISBN: 0-533-14902-9

Library of Congress Catalog Card No.: 2004092586

0 9 8 7 6 5 4 3 2 1

In memory of my mother, Mrs. Mary L. Davis,
the love of my life

Contents

Acknowledgments   ix
Introduction   xi

Love Story   1
Rolling the Dice   3
Why I Come to Church   5
Top Draft Pick   8
Vision from God   10
What Should You Have Done Yesterday?   12
What in the World are You Mad with God For?   14
I Was Stunned by the Word of God   16
Somebody's Calling My Name   18
A Time to Give   20
A Special Moment in Prayer   22
Give Till It Hurts   23
Standing in the Crossroad   24
Touched by the Spirit   27
Universal Answer   28
Who Am I Lord?   30
You Don't Get It   32
There Is a War Going On   34
See Your Breakthrough   36
Satan, You're No Match for My God   37
Before the Rooster Crows   39
Did You Do the Right Thing?   41
Look to Me   43
Mayday, Mayday, Mayday   45
Struggle   47
Who Told You That You Were Naked?   48

Child Go Play   50
What Do You Declare?   52
I'm a Witness to How God Can Take Care of You   54
Deja Vu   55
The Gospel of Mark   56
Shipwreck Faith   59
Going Home   60
What's Your Blood Type?   61
Conference Call by the Almighty God   62
Count!   64
Desperate Situation Turning Ugly   65
God's Got Him on a Leash   66
Put It Away   68
Resting Place   69
You Are Covered   71
Do You See What I See?   73
Talking to the Great Physicians   75

About the Author   77

Acknowledgments

I want to take time to thank my wife, Cheryl D. Lee, and my son, D'Angelo R. Lee, for their support and love. My pastor, Victor L. Hill, who continues to share a word of encouragement with me. And to my co-workers, Evelyn Lomax, Wanda Harris, Denise O'Neal and others, who God used, to remind me of how good and perfect His love is for me and you.

Introduction

I wrote this book because I noticed, one day in the workplace, how the people were hooked on E-mail scripture about the Word of God. It did disturb me for a moment because they were so excited about a few scriptures that someone had printed off the Internet and had passed out to them. So, I began to talk to the Lord about this matter. I needed to know what was the excitement about? When they all have a Bible in their homes and won't open it up and get more of Your word. There were no faces behind the writer's work the people were reading, yet I noticed how hungry the people were for an answer to their struggle, so I asked the Lord to allow me to put a real face behind the words they were reading. As God began to use me, my life was exposed to the lives of others around me. My past and present life was revealed to me of how God has been taking care of me. My faith was fed, as well as that of my co-workers, to know in time of my struggle of how God walked with me and protected me every day of my life. My struggle was like their struggle. So, we began to talk about the Word of God and the impact God's Word was having on us. In this book, you can understand and relate to my life, and others' lives, as God's Word is being seen in Revelation of the Holy Spirit.

THE INSPIRATIONAL VIEW OF
THE WORD OF GOD

Love Story

Sit down my child and let me talk to you. I know you think I don't hear you, but I heard you the first time you called on me early in the midnight hour of your life, with all your petitions bouncing off the throne room wall covered with tears. My child, I heard you. Attach a little faith to my word. Stand still and pray just what I say. Sit quiet and learn of me. Let me tell you a story of how much I love you. In the beginning, I shaped you like no other, blew into you my spirit, gave you life, walked with you in the mist of the garden, day and night, and when you knew you were lonely I laid you down and made you a helper so Adam would be there for you.

With Abraham I promised you a land flowing with milk and honey, but you weren't ready to possess it. That means I made you rich.

With Moses I heard your cries in Egypt and delivered you from your bondage of that hard taskmaster on your job. From the heaven I came down and parted the Red Sea and while you were in the wilderness, I fed you with manna from the heaven. On weary nights, I held you while you were holding your child. My love for you has taken you through your sickness. The doctor said I'm sorry, there's no hope for you, you won't make it through.

When those you love lied about you, I took it to the cross. When those friends saw you down and out and stepped over you, all of this I took with me to the cross for you. When you had spent your last dime and were about to lose your mind, I took it to the cross. But three days later, I got up with all the power in heaven and earth in my hand to move mountains for you.

All of my saints have been carrying my word from Genesis to Revelations. You can learn of me so open the Bible and see how much you mean to me.

Rolling the Dice

I realized one day that I have been rolling the dice all my life. In and out of relationships, thinking I found love, but to find out later I have not. Seeking to find that peace of mind that my heart has been searching for all the time, that joy which is missing. I need to fill a void in my broken heart. Moving from job to job, I can't seem to stop rolling out of one job and into another, staying a few months or staying a few years. The jobs were alright, but the pay was never enough to pay my bills. I found myself taking a chance on just about anything that came my way like the pyramid game, football board, betting on the dogs, lottery tickets, and even waging on the horses at Churchill Down's. I'm still seeking to find that thrill, yet only found heartache and bills. At the lowest point of my life, I cried out, Lord help me, please. I know I was taught in Sunday school and church what really works and by a stern word from my mother. I can still see her, on her bended knees, saying a prayer for me. Sometimes I can hear her saying, Lord, take care of my child while he is running here and there. Lord, I know now I've been rolling the dice with my life and I want to change. I can still hear my mother saying, "Child, give your life to Christ. I know he will take care of you day and night. A sure bet he hung, bled, and died for you and early the third day morning he rose for you."

Lord, I'm ready to change. I'm ready to be saved, Lord. I'm ready to give my life to You this day, just like I am win, lose, or draw. I don't want to miss the kingdom and burn in eternal fire. Many times I was on my knees rolling a set of dice and yelling, "more money, more money," trying to meet my needs instead of praying to the Lord to bless me. Lord, there are numbers I roll, 7-11, snake eyes, that caused me to get hooked. But now, Lord I'm hooked on God the Father, God the Son, God the Holy Spirit. I'm hooked on you, God, who said in six days You finished all of His Creation, and on the seventh day the word said God rested. I'm hooked, Lord, on the word about Joshua at Jericho, marching around the wall six days and on the seventh day the Lord instructed his children to shout for their victory. I'm hooked, Lord, on Your Word that said after three days in the grave, Christ rose with all power in His hand. I believe, Lord, I was included into the salvation plan. I believe, Lord, that you want me to be in good health and prosper while on this earthly journey. I believe you've already done everything that I may be saved, so here I am, Lord, broken and needing repair. Seven is a good number, Lord. Restore unto me, press down shaking together, Your love and care.

Why I Come to Church

God told Moses, congregate, symbol, gather my people to-gether. The church in our time is called. Tell my people I have seen their affliction and heard their cries. Tell them the Lord your God is going to deliver His children from their bondages, that means whatever kind of issues they have. Gather them together. I am a full service God, I guess, that shot holes in those unsaved people's reasons for not coming to church. Moses said, "Lord, who am I to tell Pharaoh and your people, you are going to deliver them from their bond-ages." Sounds like Moses is our modern day pastor, crying out to God, struggling with issues, too. God said, when you have brought the Israelites out of Egypt, you will return here to worship me at this mountain, His holy place, the church. Exodus 3-7-17, Moses said, "Lord, who shall I say sent me?" I am that I am sent me to you. The God of Abra-ham, or Isaac, and Jacob, and of Martin L. King, of Pat Rob-inson, of Jimmy Carter, deliverance is for you, just like you are, with whatever baggage you are carrying. When God said He is going to deliver you, He didn't stop there, He said I'm going to take you to a place that He is going to give you, and He is going to be your God. When I first heard the pas-tor say to the congregation, "Ask yourself, why do I come to church?" that question caused a rumbling of an earthquake in my spirit, a landslide of thoughts came pouring down in my mind. I come to worship God. Well, Mama brought me to church so I can hear about a man who can save me, and his name is Jesus. Another explosion went off in my spirit, you come because the music motivates you, the people love you, and the food is good. And you come to see who's loving who. Sometimes you come to check out the clothes, like this is a fashion show. And you wonder why people sometime won't show up. God told Moses and the leader of Israel, "Go to the King of Egypt and say let us go on a three-day journey into the wilderness to offer sacrifices to the Lord our God." Sometime you have to speak to yourself and say, "Self, no excuses today," get up and go to church and worship the Lord God today. And when you've missed too many Sundays because of work, you must go to your boss and say, I need to go to church and lay before the Lord in prayer. I've got issues and I'm in despair, I've got needs that need repair. I need to go and hook up with my brothers and sisters in prayer.

In Matthew 8-24, Anyone who listens to My teaching and obeys Me is wise, like a person who builds a house on solid rock. Though the rain comes in your life you won't collapse, because it is built on Jesus, the solid rock. Even now while you are in this promised land, there is poverty at your doorstep and in distant lands, drought, and famine, in barren land, people suffering on every hand, and yes, all these adversities are here to remind you, that I am your God who is able to take care of you.

King David tapped into something when he was a child. He said, "God delivered me from the lion, and he delivered me from the bear." You need to say this with me, "He delivered me from that car crash, from that bullet that had my name written all over it; he delivered me from drugs, he delivered me from the street, and he delivered me and you from an abusive relationship. Surely he can deliver me from this and that and anything that comes up in my life." David said, in Psalm 103, "Bless the Lord, o my soul: and all that is within me." Psalm 95, O come, let us sing unto the Lord: let us make a joyful noise to rock of our salvation. Psalm 105, O give thanks unto the Lord; call upon His

Name: make known His deeds among the people. Why do I go to church? I guess I answered that. I need to sing praises unto the Lord and bless His name, for he has been good to me. I know because He woke me up this morning. Sing with me, He keeps blessing me as the songwriter wrote, "Over and over He keeps blessing me." I've got to take the time to glorify the Lord today.

Top Draft Pick

In the sports arena, athletes are called blue-chippers. Top draft picks, which give them great status among the sports world, with wealth unimaginable to the hourly worker. Yet, peace and happiness seem to slip out of their reach. The Beatles used to sing a song: "Money Can't Buy Me Love" and that's the truth. They sign contracts that covers them three to twenty years, if they are lucky. In the Christian world, we are greater because we are heirs to the Kingdom and to the promises of God, and we have an eternal covenant. But there is one problem, we didn't read the contract to find out what is available to us. Athletes make sure what is in their contracts and receive a fat bonus before they put on a uniform to go to battle. But on the other hand, Christians gave their lives to Christ which made them available to all of the kingdom's wealth and power to put Satan under their feet. Man, that's great! That's something to shout about and stand the test of time. But one problem. We won't read the contract.

A question was asked by the pastor, "Do you know what is available for you in the word of God?" Think about it. Do you know? If you are sick and can't get well, do you know what the contract said? Too broke and can't go anywhere? Do you know what God said to Abraham that caused him to leave for the promised land? Genesis 12-1-3, You are restless and can't sleep for worrying over situations you can't control or meet. Did you read about Jesus on a ship with his disciples in the midst of a storm, being tossed and driven and couldn't see land? O, ye of little faith. Peace be still. Out of his mouth, a word of truth was spoken for me and you. When you think you got a right to be mad and raise all kinds of hell, what did your contract say about forgiveness? You may find out that God said "If you won't forgive your brother, I can't forgive you." Search your heart and your mind. Search the Word of God and see if you really know what's available in these perilous times, in God's contract with us He gave us a guarantee. His word and swore on it. And signed it with the blood of Jesus who redeemed us on Calvary. You can't make a fruitcake without reading the recipe to make sure that all that is listed goes in it to get the best result. To get the best result for your life, you must read the contract.

Vision from God

O eyes, O eyes, what do you see? God's creation in front of me.

O eyes, O eyes, what do you see? Flowers, trees, and mountains in front of me.

O eyes, O eyes, what do you see? People in a hurry who won't slow down to see. Just like Moses with the children of Israel, standing at the Red Sea.

O eyes, O eyes, what do you see? As I journey through the streets, there is more distress and loneliness I guess I see. Yet, I am reminded in time of trouble, God is my rock, God is my peace, and my strength, as the 23rd Psalm said, "the Lord is my shepherd."

O eyes, O eyes, what do you see? This land with trees and creatures still doing just what God created them to do. That's what brings a smile to me, you see. Yet, all of this God said he made for me. I do see God's word is really True, His word will not return to him void. God promised that to me.

O eyes, O eyes, what do I see? A lack of love and respect for others. Murders, terrorist attacks in the land, war talk is the plan. Yet, I am reminded again, God said, "If my people are called by My name will humble themselves and pray, I will heal the land."

O eyes, O eyes, do you see God's plan for man? He said in the beginning, "Let us make man in our image after our likeness and I gave him dominion on the earth."

O eyes, O eyes, what do you see? There is a cross for you and me.

O eyes, O eyes, what did God see? Just what He said, so,

I can speak and see what he said to me. So I can change what I do see or don't see through prayer.

In these times and seasons, I see prayer is for me.

What Should You Have Done Yesterday?

I was struck by this question I noticed on a roadside sign, and I could not get it out of my mind. So, like a computer, I ran a systems check on my mind to see what I could find. First, I remember, I did not pay my Mastercard bill on time. Whether or not I received it or put the bill from my mind. But, that's not why I'm troubled by this sign.

The second worry that came up, the trash man came, and I didn't set the trash out in time, the dog had not been fed, and cutting the grass, I know, I should have done. But in my mind, all of this is not why I'm troubled by the words on that sign.

The third thing that flashed on the computer screen of my mind is when I rose from my bed, I did not thank the Lord for seeing me safely through the night. I did not say: Lord, what do you want to do today? Instead, my mind was stuck on my family, my job and Christmastime, and the spirit spoke to my mind. All of this you did and did not do, but this is not why this sign is troubling you.

In Colossians 3:13, forebearing one another, and forgiving one another, if any man have a quarrel against any; even as Christ forgave you, so also do ye.

Verse 22, Servants, obey in all things your masters, according to the flesh; not with eye service, as men pleasures; but in singleness of heart, fearing God. O, that's why my mind and spirit are not at peace, the error of my ways has not been corrected. I must go back and un-do what I have left un-done so God can hear me when I pray and return to me his peace, love, and grace which I yearn to have each and every day.

Lord, please give me the right words to say, because in my mind I think I was wrong in this situation. Over two thousand years ago, Christ went to the cross, hung, bled, and died for all of the wrong in the world. But he got up on the third day morning and went back to see his disciples that he so loved, just to tell them the word of the Lord. Matthew 28:18–20.

What in the World Are You Mad with God For?

God said this modern generation parallels the generation of old. They dance, sing, and shout unto Me, yet they don't really know me. They've heard, they've read about Me, just like the people I delivered out of Egypt. My spirit is not real in their hearts.

God said My people are amazing, I listen to them crying out to me about their situations in their lives, Lord, move this, Lord, I need this, Lord if you don't help me, I'm, going to die. Lord, this pain is too hard for me to bear. But My people have a short memory of Me. When I move too fast and bring them out of their dilemma, I can hear them saying, my lucky ship came in on time. And when I bring them out slowly, they say to themselves, I worked it out. And the very first time the enemy has your back up against the wall, you panic, and cry out to me, Lord, help me, I don't know what to do. Exodus 14-11-12. The people turned to Moses complaining loudly, "Why did you bring us out here to die in the wilderness? Weren't there enough broken families living on the street? I could have stayed with my drunken, drugged-out husband, he only beat me once a week. Why did you make me leave? I'm on welfare and can hardly eat. I was better off living and dying on the street. Exodus 14-13. But Moses, the Pastor, told the people, "Don't be afraid. Just stand still where you are and watch the Lord rescue you. Stand on His Word, and watch God move. The adversities you see today, the problems that have you bound today, you won't see them again. The Lord himself will fight

14

for you. The Lord said to Moses, "Why are you crying unto me? Tell the people to go forward, speak My Word so the Red Sea in their lives will dry up, and cause them to cross over on dry land. Are we like Job who stood against his friends and wife declaring, I will not curse God and die? Are you like Job who asked God to just tell him why these afflictions are coming against you? My baby died, my house burned down, the stock market crashed and I lost all that I had. God said, "Sit down and let me ask you a question, and if you can answer any one of them, I will answer yours," Job 38-1-41, 39-1-30, 40-1-24, 41-1-34. Job answered God in 42-1-6, "I know that you can do anything, and that no thought can be withheld from thee." Job didn't stop there, he said, "I have heard about You before, but now I have seen You with my own eyes. I take back everything I said, and I sit in dust and ashes to show my repentance." What are you mad with God for? Didn't you know that Christ hung and bled on the cross, and before He died, He looked up and said Father, Father, forgive them, for they know not what they do. And early the third day morning, He rose for me and you.

I Was Stunned by the Word of God

When I was a child, yellow jackets, bees, and wasps caused me a lot of heartache and pain. Each time I had an encounter with my enemy, they left me in torment and in fear, swollen and in tears. I would get healed and go right back into the same situation. I know how a drug addict, an alcoholic, and a battered woman feel. When they find themselves returned to the same situation in their lives, they know they need to leave and run in another direction. After a while, we think less of ourselves and feel there is no way out. When I was stung, I covered my eyes, and took off running, couldn't see where I was going, falling down, rolling in the mud, crying out for someone to help me. Mother was there, to embrace me and handle all my care. She would say, "Mama loves you, and God does too." When I began to get older and learn what God said about me in His Word, I was stunned to find out what God said, He made me a little lower than the angel, and that my adversary belonged under my feet.

I was reminded since I am Abraham's seed, I am covered under the same covenant, and when Jesus hung, bled, and died on the cross, He made it possible for me to be called a child of God, and, early the third day morning, Jesus got up with all power in His hand.

He gave me the Holy Spirit, the same spirit that moved in place in the beginning, Genesis 1:2, to redo the world that was void of His presence. Again, when God spoke in Genesis 1:2–31, He saw what He said, so I know now I can say what God said, and I can see my deliverance. Healing is mine, peace is mine, and everything that comes against me, I cast it out in the name of Jesus. I'm no more on the run. When I speak, I spray the Holy Ghost over my situation. The word said if God be for you, who can stand against you.

Somebody's Calling My Name

I was sitting in the kitchen in my favorite place, watching TV, when my son came running in and spoke such a revelation to me. "Daddy, you called me?" I guess you know what my response was. "No I didn't call you, and if I did, you would not have come this fast. What have you done?" "Daddy, I just thought you called me to eat." I knew then, my reply was not the right one.

My mind shifted to Adam in the Garden. I can hear God saying, "Adam where are you?" Genesis 3:8–12. Like we are today, wanting to tell our story first, not ready to listen. I messed up. He made me do that. I was just there. I didn't do anything. God said there is a price you have to pay. Genesis 3:14–21.

My mind shifted again to Eli and Samuel. I Samuel 3:4–8. When Samuel was lying down in the temple of the Lord where the ark of God was, when he heard a voice call out to him, he thought it was Eli and came running to see what Eli wanted. Again and again, "It was not me that called you," Eli said. Something happened with Eli. He reflected back on his relationship with God and realized that it was God who was calling Samuel. Eli said, "Samuel, go back and lie down, and when you hear that voice again, you speak, Lord. Your servant is listening." At that point, I realized that call was for me, not for my son. God said, "Wake up and listen to those around you. Slow down and pay close attention to my children that I have placed in your care." God sometimes calls us into the ministries to teach, preach, to stand at the door and greet those you meet, and sometimes God will call you to pray for others. God may call you and instruct you to hold your peace, or just to say shut up. A storm broke in my spirit, and old spiritual song sprung forth that caused me to start singing, "Somebody's calling my name. O sinner, why don't you answer. Somebody's calling my name."

I know Lazarus was glad when Jesus called his name. He got up. Will you answer when God calls you? 1 John 11:43–45. Will you get up from your dead situation and bless the Lord?

A Time to Give

Thanksgiving and Christmas brings out the best in us. We find the time to bless others in times of need; we share our dinner plate in November, dressing the tree with lights and ornaments in December, to prepare the hearts of men for a day of giving with gifts that bring such great joy to all. But I can see much more than that. Good will, your presence, and your time for others are needed throughout the year. God gave us life long ago, with his presence. And the Lord our God planted a garden eastward of Eden. The word said, in Genesis 2:7–8, "And place man in it with food and running water," and in the midst of the garden God planted the Tree of Life, and the Tree of Knowledge of Good and Evil. And gave man instruction, "You can eat off every tree of the garden, but the Tree of Knowledge of Good and Evil. Don't eat of it." And God went on explaining to Adam, "On that day you do eat off the Tree of Good and Evil, you will surely die."

God gave us men and women like Abram. With an expression of his love, God gave Abram a promise. The Lord made covenant with Abram, in Genesis 15:8–21, saying "Unto your seed I give this land," and as time went on, God saw it was time for the Saviour to be born into the world. The angel named Gabriel was sent to Nazareth to a virgin named Mary to give her good news. Unto Mary, a child will be given, Luke 1:30–31, and his name shall be called Jesus, verse 32, and he shall be called the son of the highest, and the Lord God shall give unto him the throne of his father David.

In Matthew 3:1–2 John the Baptist was given to the

world to preach repentance, and the coming of Christ. And in Matthew 3:11, John stated "I baptize you with water but there is one who is coming after me, that is mightier, who will baptize you with the holy ghost and with fire.

In Matthew 11:25–28 Jesus gives a prayer of thanksgiving. Yes, understanding of giving is so greatly needed in this season of giving. In Matthew 14:15–21 Jesus fed five thousand. In Matthew 15:28 Jesus granted a woman's request because of her great faith. In verse 30 Jesus healed many people and fed four thousand more. It's time to give God the glory and the honor that is due to Him. We give it to Santa Claus. We sing and praise his Name. "Then one foggy Christmas eve, Santa came to say, Rudolph with your nose so bright, won't you guide my sleigh tonight," and all the reindeer will love you. I know you've heard that before, and you might be singing it right now. But did you hear that Jesus was paraded from judgment hall to judgment hall? The Lamb who knew no sin was convicted for our sins. Do you know on Calvary Cross, Jesus hung, bled, and gave up his life for you and me? But he got up on the third day morning with all power in heaven and in earth in his hand, to give us the power and authority to heal, to forgive, to give love, even when we feel we don't want to. Can you see Christ hanging on the cross? He stopped dying for a moment and said, "Father, forgive them, for they know not what they do." This is the time, your time, early in the morning, we all ought to give God thanks. Late in the midnight hour, you all should thank the Lord. It's your time, and that time is now. Give god the glory.

A Special Moment in Prayer

Praise and worship was coming to a close with the anointing filling up the house. A mother went to her knees in praise and worship. In the midst of emptying her heart to God, her child appeared in concern, yet he stood and studied the emotion of his mother, never once interrupting her as if he had determined that this was not a cry of sadness nor of danger. Just maybe this child had been exposed to prayer in the home. Moments later, the young child kneeled down and placed his hand on hers, still quiet. He was letting her know he was there for her. Another member kneeled down to join her. The young child's expression never changed, as if he knew his mother was having a one-on-one communication with God.

Oh how powerful this moment was. Non-believers could have become believers. Both of the young ladies stood up and embraced each other in fellowship and went to their seats. The young child stood to his feet with his hands stretched out to be embraced. Not a word was spoken. I reached out for him but that was not what he wanted. He waited for the embrace of his mother. She noticed her child with his hands stretched out, she reached for her child and embraced him in her arms, and not a word was said. The minister of the hour took the podium and began to speak from Psalm 122:1–27, giving God some praise in the house.

Give Till It Hurts

Something special happened tonight during the first revival of a new millennium year. . . . It was time to give unto the Lord. The Pastor asked us to give as our heart leads us. As we know, quality ministry costs, so prepare to give and be blessed. Then a moment of silence filled the house as purses and wallets began to open. And then the giving began. One by one money went into the tray, yet there was one who stood out as she struggled to pull her dollar bills out of her purse to give. The Deacon waited with a smile on his face knowing this one was truly giving from her heart. She only had play money, but the gift was real, it came from her heart. Even though she was last to come up, I believe her giving meant more to God than all the giving in the house. God said the first shall be last and the last shall be first. Then it is true, you can't beat God's giving no matter how you try. Yet we can learn from a child to give until it hurts and watch God's blessings and not worry about how he's going to do it. Matthew 18:1–4.

Standing in the Crossroad

Lord, I've been waging a war in my mind that's been going on for a long time now. I wake up the way I lay down, wondering why I'm still here. I feel like I'm standing in the crossroad of my life, wondering whether to give up or to go on. Lord, I cry out for direction.

Lord, teach me, show me how to rise up over my trouble, as our nation's standing in the crossroad, making plans for war or peace. Surely this is a stressful time for me. I find myself looking back on my life and counting more downs than ups. Even when I was a child, I noticed more downs than ups. Like the three times when we got burned out of our home and a day before being put out of another. Suddenly a calm breeze filled the room of my spirit and a voice spoke to me and said, "Do you also remember it was cold and I housed you? And the day the rent office said you would be put out into the street, I was there. Yes, I remember the family next door got set out that same day. My child, do you think they were too tired to set you out, too?" Oh, I see, Lord, that had to be you. "Each time you were sitting under the Word when Satan's fiery dot struck your house, I was there to clothe and feed you, and place a roof over your head." But Lord I'm old now, and weary, and each morning I pray and leave for work, and all of my troubles follow me down the road. I feel sometimes like I need to keep on driving. Yet, which direction should I take? As the road signs appear in front of me, 20 East, 59 North, Exit Ahead, Slow Down, 60 is the speed limit and I'm driving 70, as my life of trouble carries me in all directions. Up ahead of me, my headlights break a path in the morning darkness as I travel

into the dark, winding, curved roads where I cannot see. Lord, do you have an answer for me?

"My child, Jesus' suffering was foretold in Mark 10:32–34 about the road he must take for your sake. Even in the garden of Gethsemane in Matthew 26:38–42, Jesus grieved about his crossroad, but said to his Father, if this cannot pass away unless I drink, thy will be done. And when Jesus was betrayed and led from Judgment Hall to Judgment Hall for your sake, and while Christ was hanging on the cross between two robbers, with those passing by hurling abuse at him, in Matthew 27 38:40, Jesus was at his crossroad. But Jesus stayed there. He looked to his left and to his right. He looked down, He looked up, but didn't come down because He knew who He was, the son of the living God, the sacrifice Lamb of God, so he died and rose on the third day just like he said, with all power in His hand. My child, Christ finished it, so when you do not know which way to go, pray what he said, follow his ways, follow my teachings, as the Holy Spirit guides you through this earthly journey."

Touched by the Spirit

Have you ever woken up in the morning ready to start a new day? Or opened your eyes and just knew that you didn't need to go anywhere that day? And thinking to yourself what kind of mess is waiting for me? Why not say to your spirit: "Lord, I'm excited to see what you're going to do today"? Thinking there are some people you want to meet, and some you don't want to see. Guess what spirit latched on to me? As I walked by, I could hear words spoken that didn't bless me. He surely looked mad to me, and another would say, what's wrong with you? Yet I held back my steam. Just like all volcanos, if the pressure and stress of life is not released, you will eventually explode around people. But early in the morning I was met by another spirit that brought love and peace to me. And when she spoke to me, she offered prayer, not gossip, not even the right to be mad, you see. As a shaking and trembling went from my hand to my feet, God's presence reached out and steadied me. O mighty man of God, peace in your spirit that passes all understanding, reach to the heavens and sing praises to me. Joy does come in the morning as my spirit touches you from the dead and wakes you out of a deep sleep. So shout praises as you stand to your feet, King David reminded me in Psalm 103, "Bless the Lord, O my soul: and all that is within me bless his holy name."

Bless the Lord, O my soul, and forget not all his benefits.

I was touched by King David again out of Psalm 107 that left no room to be sad. My spirit began to sing, "O give thanks unto the Lord, for he is good; for his mercy endures forever." Yes, I am touched by a new spirit of praise.

Universal Answer

God said something to me while on the way to work: no weapons formed against me shall prosper. God said, praise me all day long, and so I broke out in song. No weapons formed against me shall prosper; no, it won't work. I was filled up from my mind to my heart, and my soul was on fire. I was caught up in the spirit, like a drug addict would say, I'm flying high, and I'm on cloud nine. And if I was in the midst of the disciples on the day of the Pentecost, you would have said I was drunk with wine. Acts 2:1. All morning long, God's word was in my spirit and if anyone got too close, they got the same words I was singing: no weapons formed against me shall prosper. Isaiah 54:17. God said spread the word, so everyone got an earful of bad singing, but God's spirit began to transfer to the hearts and minds of everyone who was close to me. Those close got infected by the Holy Ghost. I could see the transfer, peace was in the place, yet for three to four hours I kept singing and had God's word on my mind. When I couldn't sing anymore, the devil tried to slip into my mind and change my thought pattern with the cares of this world. Even when people-problems came up, I had the same answer for them that I was not able to sing anymore. So I spoke it, no weapons, no weapons formed against you shall prosper; no, it won't work, it won't work. If you're sick it won't work; if you're struggling with a loved one, it won't work; your bills about to take you out, it won't work; and on and on I went until God released me. The word I got truly is a universal answer. God said he will do just what he said; he will stand by his word. Open your spiritual eyes and see your struggles that surround you, then look again and see God has surrounded your problem. II Kings 6:16. I opened a letter that was hand-carried from a friend to a friend that blessed me. Inside the letter was a bookmark with a cross and an inscription from Psalms 91. It lets me know I've got security; I'm safe because I trust in the Lord. So see your struggles, and all that you are going through, and then see what God said about your struggles and watch God move.

Who Am I Lord?

High turbulence, take flight like an eagle, mighty man of God, I started looking around to see where that came from, and who was wearing that cape, but no superman was there. Chosen child of the kingdom, get up. Lord, you just pulled me out of the mud pit. The stain and smell of where I've been has kept me from rising above my past. Someone is always there to remind me where I've been. I'm just glad I am not a politician, and then the whole world would know where I've been. At a mature age, I considered myself grown and left home, out from under your covenant. I am the one who wanted to leave the church and do whatever I wanted. Why Lord is it, you love me so much? "In the beginning, my child I said let us make man in our image, after our likeness, male and female, and have dominion over everything in the air, land, and the seas, and he blessed man and gave them a set of conditions." Genesis 1:28–29. That's good to know, that I was not just put out here blind and stumbling around.

How special you said I was, Lord? Genesis 2:7. "And the Lord God formed man from the dust of the ground, and he breathed into his nostrils the breath of life and I became a living soul. I know he said man, but this brain said he was talking about me. Even when I hear a word from God, whether it's over the pulpit, or over the airwaves, I feel God's words are talking about me. Oh Adam, get up, get out of the mud and go home. Let our supernatural God plan our life for us, because every day I need a fresh word that only he can provide for me. This brain is not able to see. I said to myself the first superman was Adam on Earth because of the love connection between God and man. Being close to God, there is nothing you can't do. Genesis 2:19. God said he formed every beast of the field and every fowl of the air, and out of the ground he brought them to Adam to see what he would call them. Adam's brain had to be running on a supernatural cell. Everything Adam's brain said, that's what it was. I realize that God blew that same seed into me that caused Adam to see what he said, so I can call on my turbulent situation to breed life from my spirit mind by activating the seed of God embedded in my soul with the world of God. Who am I, Lord? Luke 14:11–24. My lost child that I now call my mighty man of God, my superman, the one I cleaned up, the one who's finance is at death's door, the one that needed me day and night, that same one Jesus went to the cross and to the grave and got up on the third day morning with all power in heaven and Earth in his hand to give back to me his supernatural power the Holy Ghost close in his authority. You can rise above. Proverbs 3 and 4 will bless you.

You Don't Get It

God said something to me, "You are caught up in a wave of disobedience, and if I don't get you out of it, Jonah, you are going to drown." I heard that, Lord. I'm mad now. First, you called me, what? Peter? And now you call me Jonah. That's why I called on you in the first place, Lord, because they were calling me depressing names and have been giving me hell, and here you go, Lord doing the same thing. "My child, you don't get it. Forgive. Forgive those who hurt you. You are standing in the way. Forgive." I can't do that, Lord. This hurt goes way back. "Love your enemy, Jonah." I can't do that, Lord. You can't send me to them. I don't want to forgive. Jonah 1:1–3. "My child, there is no peace or deliverance until you do." Lord I have said in my heart I would rather die before I forgive them. Lord, I've been waiting on you to take them out. If I forgive them, Lord, I know you will, too.

"Jonah, you don't get it. Like I told Lot, you are holding me up, you are in the way. Forgive so I can straighten this mess up." Genesis 19:13. I need to get you out of the land of un-forgiveness. Don't look back, you still don't get it. I need you out of the valley of your rocky past. Judgment is mine, said the Lord.

May I remind you, my child, Jesus was talked about, lied on, and called an evildoer, in John 18:17–18–19.

And even Pilate wrote an inscription and put it on the cross. And it was written, "Jesus the Nazarene, the King of the Jews," and looking back, the King of Egypt that met me at the Red Sea called me the Hebrew God, true and living God, I am God Almighty. The Lily of the Valley and the

Bright and Morning Star. Even King David called me in Psalm 109 the God of my praise.

"Oh," what my ears have heard. I get it now. Thank you, Lord.

There Is a War Going On

I say to you, Lord, be patient with me, I don't want you to be mad at me. I just need to know what in the world is going on. I'm your child, you created me for your pleasure, I know you want me to live and not die. I prefer to have tears of joy, than tears of struggle. Lord, let me tell you my story while I'm down on my knees. I peer out my window and marvel at your goodness spread from sunrise to sunset, out on this earth, just like broken glass. My peace was shattered by the presence of gunfire that filled the air, blasting sirens from a fire truck racing to a direction I knew not where.

My first thought: neighbors against neighbors or brothers against brothers, trying to take each other out, as the rapid gunfire filled the sky.

There's nothing good I hear in these ears. I'm bombarded by my family, my friends, my next of kin, my job, and even the school is calling me with their mess. And now I'm waiting on the doctor's call to read me my medical test.

God began to speak. "My child is complaining so loud he can't hear me speak. The Pastors have been blowing the trumpet throughout the land to warn the people there is no peace, there is a war going on, a natural war and a spiritual war, that is being waged in this world. As the artillery shells of sin are bursting in the mountains, and on the valley floor, the spirit of infirmity stretching out greater than all the seas. Mortar blasts of anger and hatred, resting in the valley of the mind, on the terrain in the hearts of men. A spirit of immortality is heard on the radio, and seen on most, if not all, TV stations, from Ephesians 6:10–18. Finally, be strong in the Lord, and in the strength of his might. Put on the full armor of God, that you may be able to stand firm against the schemes of the devil. Special note for the saint, read Daniel 9-10-11-12.

See Your Breakthrough

The Word of God continues to remind us that we are the children of God. Like all children, we need help to determine what is right and wrong. Even when we need to see something happen, that's where our Daddy comes in. If our Earthly Father promises something to us, we do not question it, we believe it until he fails us. But Christ said, "Let not your heart be troubled, believe in God, believe also in Me," in John 14:1–2. Use your imagination for a moment. You've got to see God and his love for you. Picture yourself moving around in this natural world, needing a breakthrough. You see no way out. But God said the Earth is the Lord and the fullness thereof and all that dwell therein is His. We must first look for a spiritual breakthrough before a natural breakthrough can happen. Pretend by faith that you can see a circle of God's love all about you. Healing is above you, deliverance is off to the right of you, prosperity in front of you, and at your feet, God's love for you. Forgiveness is off to the left of you, all that you need is within arm's reach. Reach out, grab it, and stand on God's Word about that need in your hands. Believe it by faith, and say what God said, "That is the true answer for seeing your breakthrough." Don't look first with your natural eye. If you ask a woman or a man, they would say that's not what I thought I saw. Use your spiritual eyes that are connected to the heart of God. Don't wait for once a year on an angel to come down and trouble the water to get a breakthrough. When Jesus said, "Believe in me."

Satan, You're No Match for My God

I'm looking for a new agency that can handle me with the power of truth and love. Satan, I know now I've been giving you too much credit. Satan, you took me to the top of the world and showed me what you had to offer me, and I took the bait. It is clear to me now, Satan, that I was blessing you by staying out all night, spending every dime I made in the name of enjoyment, and wearing out my covenant union with my mate. Satan, you pushed me into my place of adversity by placing your thoughts into my mind and causing me to be in a suicidal state. I was pacing back and forth in my living room and unearthed the greatest treasure of all time. Lying there on my coffee table, buried in dust, the Holy Bible. The spoken Word of God. I became an archaeologist that day. I wiped back the dust and opened up to Isaiah 14:9–22, and un-covered that, Satan, you're no match for my God. I've seen what happens to you, but I needed to see more and found myself reading Job 1:1–5. Job and his family were having a good time, a party. I can relate to that, so I kept reading from Job 1:6–7 where the sons of God came and presented themselves before the Lord, and also Satan. And God asked Satan, where are you coming from, and what have you been doing? I yelled out, Lord, he's been here in the midst of your child, Lord, deceiving and causing all kinds of hell. Lord, I remembered how my mate use to meet me at the front door, asking me, "Where have you been? And what have you been doing?" My God, they already knew. I continued reading the book of Job and each event got deeper in my soul and spirit, to the point I was yelling out Loud, "Satan you're no match for my God. You can't give what you ain't got." In Job 42:5, Job said, "I had heard about you before, but now I have seen you with my own eyes." I know now, Job was singing that spiritual song we are singing today, Lord, have your way, have your way Lord . . . blessed be the name of the Lord. . . . Satan, I have found my way out, and it's through the Word of God.

Before the Rooster Crows

Before the rooster crows, where did I hear that from? It's got to mean something to me because it keeps coming up in my mind. OK, let me think, before the rooster crows. Oh yes, in Matthew, Jesus said one of you will betray me, and Peter, you will deny me, Matthew 26:34. Jesus said unto him, "Verily I say unto thee, That this night, before the cock crows, thou shall deny me thrice." Lord, are you calling me Peter? Are you saying that I am denying you in some way? How Lord? Jesus said sit, stay here. Watch with me while I go and pray, but each time I return, you are asleep, or too tired, to pray and stay awake with me.

Lord, I was at Wednesday night's Bible Study, and faithful in attending Sunday school, and staying all day for regular service, and you know I attend all church programs. But child, each day and night I watch over you, it was my grace and mercy that brought you through, and all you give me is a quick thank you, Lord, and you are on your way. You did not set aside time for me, nor put me first. Could you not pray to me one hour each day? You lift me up at church and lay me down at work. The world doesn't know who you are. In Matthew 26:40–41, Jesus said, "Then he returned to the Disciples and found them asleep." Lord, are you saying that you want me to be committed to prayer? Spend time in prayer. The place of God in your heart can only be rebuilt by the Word of God. You denied me when you didn't put me first, you denied me because you are too busy to pray each day. You speak at me, and don't wait to hear what I've got to say. Before the rooster crows, that's all you need to know. Judgment is at your door; you can't walk away, nor rest today.

Did You Do the Right Thing?

A day late and a dollar short, this is the way my life was going until I finally reached my point of no return. My greatest fear had been realized, to be cut off from the presence of the Lord. If you've ever been given a final notice that you will be cut off and you knew the money is not there, and you try to put it off to a later date, and one day you try to turn the knob, or flick the switch, or better yet, pick up the phone and get no dial tone, you really get sick of begging and borrowing from everyone you know to a point where they hate that they know you. Lord, I have a lot of concern. You see, I've been down on my knees praying and praying and trying to reach you, but I get no return answer. I feel cut off from your presence. Are my words getting through to you? Lord, Jesus said when he was in his deepest hour, he prayed. Lord, I know you always hear me when I pray.

Lord, I even prayed in the name of Jesus. At that very moment a question came back at me. Did you do the right thing? Is there something in your past or present that may be preventing your prayer from getting through?

Well, Lord, me and my co-worker and my boss don't get along very well. I have not forgiven them. "My child," it is written, in Colossians 3:13, barring with one another, and forgiving each other, whoever has a complaint against anyone; just as the Lord forgave you, so also should you. And Ephesians: 4:32, Mt. 6:14. But Lord, the way I was treated, it's hard to forgive. It's just hard. My child in Luke 23:34, Jesus, your redeemer said, "Father, forgive them, for they know not what they do. My child, this you must have heard, from Mark 11:26, but if you do not forgive, neither will your

Father who is in heaven forgive your transgressions. So, you are saying, Lord, you can't hear me because I have not done the right thing. I see now it was me who disconnected my prayer line to you, Lord. No healing, no prosperity, and no peace. I must go back and ask my co-worker and my boss to forgive me and set me free so my God can hear me when I speak. I've got needs that won't be met until I straighten up my mess. I've got to go back and do the right thing.

Look to Me

God said something to me one day when I was in Wal-Mart Super Store with my wife. My child, you are struggling, not because you want to get off your feet, you feel out of place. "Oh yes, Lord." The first turn I make I'm in the woman's section where there are personal things, large and small. So my struggle goes on. I'm trying to hurry and get out of this area, but that doesn't work, and sometimes she may turn to me and ask, "What do you think?" My answer isn't going to come out right because I'm struggling. God said look to see me in your entire struggle. How, Lord? You saw items on the shelf, but look again; I see large, small, and different shapes of people that need assistance from the Lord. In the baby section, pull-ups of all kinds, large and small, but what do you think their cry to me is going to be? Lord, many of your children are going to need you to pull them out of their mess. Look to see me, child. Well, Lord, the next aisle carries medicine, large and small, many types for different reasons. I am the God, who is able to heal all sickness and diseases. Luke 6:12–13. I am able to raise you from the dead. Keep looking to see me, child. Ahead is hardware, garden equipment to labor with, after I've tilled the ground of your mind with my word and up-rooted you from sin, you can spring forth and bear great fruit. I'm in the glass and plate area, Lord. Oh, how fragile your heart is. Any little wind can blow, and you'll break up and all your hope will be shattered. But I can keep you in perfect peace if your mind stays on me. You can walk through the valley of the shadow of death and fear no evil. Psalm 23. I see, Lord, let me try this one. I'm in the clothes section. You can provide for me every day like you provided for the children that wandered in the wilderness for forty years. Deuteronomy 2:7. So surely you can take care of me. You feed me when I'm hungry and clothe me when it's needed. Grocery shopping has taken on a new meaning for me and now I'm in the food area, where all that's good and perfect comes from you. I remember one of the disciples said unto Jesus, "It's getting late in the evening and this is a desert place, we don't have food to feed the multitude of people, we need to send them away." But on that day, you fed five thousand men plus women and children. Matthew 14:15–21. Your answer for me, Lord, is whatever I'm going through, look to see you in all things.

Mayday, Mayday, Mayday

I'm going through, stressed out over my dilemma. Does God really hear me? I thank God for our global communication satellite system, the mobile phone, and the belt-held beeper, so when we have fallen and can't get up an emergency signal goes out to the satellite to make a call to someone on the ground to send help to your location. When a ship is caught in a violent storm, a mayday goes out before the ship goes down to alert someone of their last location and to send help. When an airplane loses an engine or a hijacker is on board, a distress signal goes out to someone on the ground to receive its last location before the signal stops. One problem with this system, you've got somebody on the ground that may reach you in time, but may not be able to save you in time. But the Bible said Martha and Mary sent out a distress call to Jesus that their brother Lazarus was sick, whom they loved. But Jesus proclaimed Lazarus' sickness is not unto death. No, it's for the glory of God. Oh, he may not come when you want him, but he will be on time. Don't let people tell you it's too late, or the doctor tell you you may only have six months to a year to live. Send your mayday to the Lord and allow him to raise up your dead situation. John 11:25–26. Jesus told Martha, I am the resurrection and the life, he who believes in me, even though he was dead, yet shall he live. When your enemy is trying to take you out, you need to go to your knees in prayer like the Hebrew boys did, before they were thrown into the fiery furnace, and say to your enemy or your sickness, I shall live forever. The Lord will take care of me, and if he doesn't, I know he can. God even told Moses at the burning bush, I heard the cries of my people in Egypt and I'm going to send you, Moses, to deliver a message of deliverance to Pharaoh that he is not going to hear.

But I will deliver them. Exodus 3:7–9. The Holy Spirit is our global satellite system which is in us now, instead of hovering over us as a mighty escort. Just call on Jesus and tell him what you want. Get the right access number from the Word of God, so when you call him up, you'll get the right answer. Daniel prayed for twenty-one days for an answer, but God said "Daniel, I heard you the first time and I sent Gabriel my Angel, but he was caught up in a spiritual battle with the Prince of Persia that blocked his way to you. So I sent Michael, one of the Archangels, to relieve him for your sake." Daniel 10:12–13. Instead of saying mayday, mayday, just say Jesus, Jesus, Father, in the name of Jesus. Plead the blood of Jesus over your situation, that's our access number. The Holy Spirit is in place to take your call. If you say back to Jesus what God said about your need, your faith will bring you peace and joy.

Struggle

Hush mind, I have put up with you all the way down the road, changing from one struggle to another. With each subject you bring up it's keeping me bound in strife. You've got me speaking out loud to myself, and someone is going to find me out.

I can't tell anybody about what I'm going through. I just don't know what to do. Unliving a lie is hard to do. Everybody thinks I've got it going on, but, Lord, you know the truth.

Talk to me, Lord, that's what I need you to do. Look around, my child, and tell me what stands out to you. Well, Lord, there is one woman sitting in a corner with her head down. She needs me. Lord, there is a woman standing in the middle of the floor laughing and talking very loud. That one needs me, too. How about this one, clean from top to bottom and sporting a new hairdo. Yes, that one needs me too. "My child, you can continue to look around, but they all need me, too. Your struggle and their struggle may not be the same, but you all are going through." So, Lord, what do we need to do? Ask for forgiveness and that's what I will do. Forgive yourself and turn your past loose. In John 6:28–29, verse 35–40, in Phillippian 4:4–8 Paul gives a final thought: Rejoice in the Lord always, and again I say, rejoice.

Who Told You That You Were Naked?

I was met in the street one day by one of my church members who spoke such encouraging words to me. How good I looked and how much I was missed. I wanted to cry out for help, but I hid myself behind closed doors, and locked myself into my work, because I was spiritually naked and well-clothed.

Moments later when I thought I was alone, a voice spoke to me and said, "Who told you that you were naked?" I waved it off, and continued to hide myself in my work. And a voice spoke to me again. "My child, who told you that you were naked? And why are you hiding from me?" My mind flashed back on Adam in the Garden in Genesis 3:11. The Lord spoke to me, have you eaten from the tree I told you not to? Yes Lord. I got caught up in the joy of this world and I did lust, and covet my brother's wife. I did steal, I did kill with the spoken word from my tongue, but who told you that you were naked? Well, Lord, I can say like David, all of my life I knew you walked with me and talked with me, and You showed me things before they happened. I used to walk boldly in this world, because I knew you loved me. I slept good at night and never worried about the passing storm in the night, or about job closings around me. Lord, I worry about everything now, so I hid myself from you. Lord, I confess, I sinned against you, I lost my covering, the Holy Spirit. Yes, you did sin against me, just like the woman that was caught in adultery and was brought to Jesus. Your sins are forgiven, go and sin no more. My son, Jesus, took all of your sins to the cross when he hung, bled, and died and rose on the three day morning, and freed you from the stain of sin. You are now clothed in the blood of Jesus.

Child Go Play

Child, go somewhere and play. Go play!!! You have heard this or said it to your child or kids, and not really understood the full scope of what you've said. When your child stood and looked at you as if he or she is saying, "What do you mean?" it should concern you. Have you ever taken the time to see where your child went to play? And if you say go outside and play and they don't want to go, you may have realized you have messed up. Go to the door, open it and look out. What do you see? The most common answer would be nothing or kids hanging on the corner with nothing to do. The first thing we want to say is kids are heading for trouble. No kids playing any type of ball, no made-up games can be seen like we used to do. We would take an old broomstick or an old tire or just an inner tube and play until the sun went down. Do you see younger kids watching older kids play? That's what we did, that's how we learned to play. No one is sitting on his or her front porch enjoying the cool fresh air. It's too hot, you can get shot sitting on your porch, are excuses we use today. We gave up being outside for air conditioning and color TV. So when we say "child go play," they go and turn the TV on, these kids never knowing really how to play. An example of what I'm saying: Providence Baptist Church invited everyone out on March 18, 2000 for a fun day flying kites. Only a few kids and a few grownups came. The kids ran with their kites into the wind, away from the wind, they ran pulling their kites into no wind, yet they had fun. If only enough people would have come out and showed them how to fly a kite, just think how much more they could have learned. More kids stayed

in than were sent out to play. Our government leaders and preachers preach that we need to take back our streets and our communities but they don't know how. It's as simple as children "go out and play," and if every household or neighbor would go out and sit and watch while they play, there would be no room for crime on the street today.

What Do You Declare?

I was cleaning up at the church when God said, "What do you declare?" What do I declare? I was puzzled about that word. I didn't know what it meant to me. I don't understand. A while later God said, "You are in this world but you are not of this world." You want to go to the Kingdom? Yes, Lord. What do you declare? I remembered the customs of other countries. They asked you on the way out, do you have anything to declare, and if you try to leave with something on you or in you, you can and will be held up and prosecuted for the illegal substance on or in you. But, Lord, what is it I'm carrying that is illegal? The Lord said you've got issues in the flesh that won't let you through. I want to take you further in me, but I've got to get Egypt out of you. There is sin in the camp of your heart. You declared in your heart that you are a child of mine, but you don't act like it. My commandment is to love your brother as you love yourself, forgive those who trespass against you. My commandment was not to kill, but you killed with the tongue instead of speaking life with it. What do you declare? My child, you are the one who's been walking on thin ice with me in this world. Don't tell me, Lord, I confess I left the top off the trash can of my mind and allowed people to bring me mess and now I have become a dumping ground. I confess I did not run for cover or send gossip away from my mind, so when they were mad I was mad too, knowing all the time their hatred would spread in me as long as I listened to it. Lord, I declare I have not studied your word enough to keep the illegal substance of sin from taking root in my mind. Lord, I should have asked you to fill my cup and let it overflow with love, peace, and joy. Lord, I have stood still and allowed immoral sin to go on un-checked in front of me, in the name of minding my own business, just as long as it stayed away from me. Lord, take everything that is not like you out of me. Help me to say what you would say and do what you would, so I can see the things of God. This is what I declare unto you, Lord.

I'm a Witness to How God Can Take Care of You

I've been in a world of hurt; I've been guided by the best, the prince of deception, and the deceiver of Adam. The same one of whom God changed his name from Lucifer to Satan.

I've got a confession to make because God's been good to me. The same faults and failures of this world, I'm guilty of the same foolishness, too. Paul said, even now evil is on every hand. When I try to do good, I find myself doing things wrong. I've concluded, too, there is no good in the flesh. But God met me one day on my knees while asking for forgiveness for my sin. Amazingly, I was accepted. God placed me in his witness protection program, and this wild olive branch has been engrafted into the body of Christ as one of his children. In the kingdom of darkness, violence erupted as a mighty volcano pushing out hatred over a soul reclaimed by Jesus, and a contract was reissued on my life. Satan declared he wouldn't sit still. If he can't control me, no one else will. That sounds like the pusher of drugs and prostitution. The pusher of hatred in the land, the author of sickness and despair, all of this is part of Satan's master plan.

In clear view God will hide me. Psalm 34:1–22. I've got reason to bless the Lord. Psalm 30:1–12. I am a witness who knows he is covered by the blood of Jesus; my laundry list of sin has been redeemed by the blood of Jesus. I have undisputed proof that it was God who woke me up and not my alarm clock that needed a power source to cause it to work. I can remind myself no weapon formed against me shall prosper. I'm a witness to how God can take care of you.

Deja Vu

French or English, I have not determined where this word came from, but the significance of it rings loud in my spirit. I've seen it somewhere because it keeps coming up in my mind. Deja vu. Is this an unwritten language or a vision we just experience over and over again? It's not just a premonition of something good or bad about to happen to us, but this warning always leaves us to say to someone else, something told me that was going to happen.

What is it, Lord? People and places, things I revisit, that have been dead and gone, keep popping up. "My child, that's nothing but the devil." The smell and the sight of things bring up pleasant and unwanted memories, like a song from the past that causes you to re-live an old relationship when those people were not on your mind, but still in the spirit of the flesh.

Deja vu. I've been here before, something told me, and I knew that was going to happen. All of the above needs to be replaced with the Holy Spirit who is reminding us there are issues dead and buried, old and new, that keep resurfacing in our lives. We have not asked God to forgive us for those things attached to those events in our lives or spirit that bring life as if they are happening that very moment, which brings joy of a good thing and moments of distress for the heartache of bad times. My emotion has been affected by the spirit of that thing. Freedom comes from forgiveness.

The Gospel of Mark

Matthew, Mark, Luke, John; these guys we know so well because of their walk with Jesus. But, this Mark attends Sunday school in a little church on the side of a hill called Providence Baptist Church. The life of Mark could easily have been written for a motion picture, as a screenwriter would say his life is on a parallel with many people in this world today. He begins to tell his life story of how he ran the streets of Georgia and the city of Birmingham, Alabama, pushing drugs in a runaway lifestyle pace that this world can test to this day. Mark was unaware that God was preparing him to do work for those who were lost and in need of spiritual care. The Bible said David was chosen by God to be King, but his training ground was the valley and fields laced with lions, bears, and sheep to prepare him to lead God's chosen people. Drugs, crime, and the streets are what God used to prepare Mark for his work in the streets, which we fail to see. God turned him around; this leaves me spellbound. The transformation was astounding, to see a man give his life to Christ and become a new creature. What was truly revealed was God's purpose for a man that he was shaping and molding for a future place and time. Mark said I've been there and done that. To a point, he was willing to give up and die for a change in his life. The question that he never had an answer for, he found through faith in the Word of God. Because of his new walk with God, the power of prayer and deliverance was in his hand. Christ Jesus walked the streets among the people, who were weary, wounded, and sometimes sad. But he brought hope, healing, and deliverance to all who were in despair. Pressing for the mark of his high calling, the chosen Lamb of God, Jesus, said it is finished. I've been there and done that, all that his Father's purpose for his people he loves so much. In Mark 10:15, Jesus said to them, "Go into the entire world preaching the gospel to all creation. Salvation is at hand, to be called to be a foot soldier is God's plan."

Shipwreck Faith

Warning sirens are going off. My day is getting darker than my night. The strong winds are blowing, shaking my raft of faith. No horizon in the distance to set my sight on to increase my faith.

How do I yell for help? Who do I yell to? How do I say to someone, I'm lost and living in a sea of people that are being tossed and driven just like me? The mailman goes up and down, all around my area, shifting side to side, turning like the mighty waves from the sea headed right for me, packing my debt in a storm cloud. My creditors won't wait nor give me rest. They offer me a life raft that puts me deeper in debt. Bills are pouring in like rain. Not enough pay to make ends meet each day.

I climb to the lowest point on my knees and begin to pray, "Lord, do you not care I'm drowning? Sinking deep in despair, hanging on by a wing and a prayer?"

O ye of little faith, peace, be still, was whispered in the storm and moved through the mighty waves to magnify my faith. God said let go, let go of your friends, they are dragging you under, hold on to me. In the midst of a storm, God granted me grace.

I began to sing an old spiritual song of victory because love lifted me; love lifted me when nothing else could help; love lifted me with friends all around me; only God's love lifted me, love lifted me; when I was sinking deep in sin, far from the peaceful shore, love lifted me.

Going Home

My mother used to say, go ahead but be back before the sun goes down and be in before the street lights come on. We didn't understand a lot of things, yet rain or shine getting home was never off our minds. Now that we are up in age. God's word reminds us that we are out here for a little while, but keep your eyes on the Kingdom of light because one day you need to go home.

The eagle knows he has to leave home and engage the struggle of life and all that it holds: the life of work, play, pleasure, and any unseen circumstances put forth by his enemy whose job is to take him out, to keep from reaching his place of safety. But we need to realize, like the eagle, in times of trouble, fly, and run to the sun, and the Son will hide you day and night because He cares for you.

The prodigal son realizes the slave worker in his father's house was living better than he was in the world, so he decided to get up and go home. Luke 15:11–18.

One day you wake up to yourself and realize Jesus is the way to the truth and the light, and that no one goes home to the Father until you confess up that you have strayed and sinned against him and ask for forgiveness.

What's Your Blood Type?

Do you know your blood type? Blood is getting low, time is running out. The Red Cross is pleading for you to step up and be counted. Accidents and tragic events are gripping the land, surgeries are being held up, and that's not the plan. Blood disease is putting a strain on blood supplies. B+, B−, A+, A−, O+, O−, and on and on, some are common blood types and some are rare, and some blood is contaminated, which adds a burden to the blood shortage in times of need. It is so amazing to me, man's blood type has changed and gone in many directions that we need help badly to survive. I'm so glad Jesus shed his blood on Calvary for our sins, sickness, heartache and pain; Jesus created a supernatural blood type which is sealed by the Holy Spirit. No, the doctor can't see it under a microscope, but prayer can see the blood of Jesus. From the foundation of the world it was written, God prepared Jesus the Lamb of God, to be slain to redeem us from sin. The First Adam caused us to fall and the second Adam, who was the First Adam in the beginning, knew no sin, hung, bled, and died, but that's not how the story ends. The Bible said three days later he got up with all power in Heaven and Earth in his hand. I was reclaimed by Jesus whose blood won't run out. It's everlasting. O, the blood has signed my name. I'm covered under Jesus' name. Blue Cross covers some things, but the blood of Jesus covers all things. My blood type is Jesus. Poke me, cut me, run your tests and inject me with what you think is best. Cast your doubts and watch God do the rest. If you know that old spiritual song, sing it with me: "O the blood, O the blood done signed my name. Jesus told me, the blood done signed my name."

Conference Call by the Almighty God

O here we go again, we've got to listen to the bottom line and I'm not going to do no more than I'm already doing.

In the business world, CEOs and upper management called their chosen people together to give them a progress report on the future of their business.

With speeches and graphic charts, they know there is a need to let the people under them know where they stand with their business plan. To encourage the faithful and send warnings to those who are not reaching their goals. But it's the Almighty God who called this meeting, so let it be known, no one can miss this call to discuss the state of His business of salvation. God said to His people who are called by His name, I'm mad. The people of this world are saying disturbing things about you, and I'm not pleased. My leaders are committing all forms of sin. My little one in the community can't even wash cars without setting a bad example. I can see, even in the workplace I can't say you are doing your work to honor me. When this world is talking about you, they are talking about me, because of your walk, and their statements, I hear so much, which is why do I need their God when they are living worse than me. God said this when I saw the progress report on this world.

My children are still dying in the street. They still don't know me. No love nor forgiveness for your brother I can see. Your praise and worship is a stench to my nostrils. Because of the lifestyle you keep, the elderly are not being attended to, because you don't have time to go by to meet them. God said, "You have messed up my name. My investment in you is not producing much of a return, but I'm going to use you

who messed it up to straighten it out." Deuteronomy 28:1–8.
"Get busy, my children, and do the work you were called
and anointed to do. You know not the day or the appointed
hour the Son of God will come."

Count!

I got a powerful word from the Lord this morning while united together in a circle of prayer with the intercessor.

I remember thinking as prayer was going forth that the number of intercessors here is great this morning. As I can feel the power of agreement taking place in the house, but in the midst of the circle I can see the power of the Lord building to an atomic stage and exploding through us, causing a burning away of our sins with the intensity of His redeeming power.

As praise and worship continued on in our spirit, I was riding the shockwave of God's redeeming power spreading throughout the land in his people, overtaking and reclaiming the inhabitants of this world.

When we dispersed to areas in the church to kneel and pray, I couldn't sit still due to the traveling spirit of grace carrying me out to show me God's mercy and saving grace.

The moment I did sit still, God said count, from the back of the room, to the front and across the room my eyes went, counting God's gifts to the church. Ten, I said to myself, and that's not enough. The word came again, Twelve. Count! Ten I counted again, and the spirit allowed me to see there are two that are not here that must be counted, too. There we are twelve chosen intercessors God called to unite for work of this ministry in this house. Count your blessings. Name them one by one. Count your many blessings and see what the Lord has done.

Desperate Situation Turning Ugly

Death is so powerful to a loved one; especially the loss of a child or a mother or to the one you've bonded close to from the beginning of your life.

When you are faced with insurmountable odds, and death is on the horizon that you fear so much, you find stress is about to take you out and an inner cry consumes your heart. You begin to doubt God and turn away from your faith, and all the crying in the world won't change anything to go your way. Yet deep from the inside of your soul, you ask God a question, "Why, Lord?" When petitioning God for a change, a last-hour reprieve, hoping God will step in and change the death sentence to life.

God said something to me early one morning as I was listening to a woman whose mother's journey on this Earth was about to end. God said, as he heard the woman cry from her heart, "tell her she was mine first and that her loss will hurt, but I grieve, too." Death is just a gate we all have to pass through. Have peace in knowing that Jesus died on the cross so the other door would be opened for you and me.

John 14:1–3. Let not your heart be troubled: ye believe in God, believe also in me.

In my Father's house are many mansions; if it were not so, I would have told you. I go to prepare a place for you.

It's good to know you can call on the Lord and get an answer that will bring peace in the midst of a storm.

God's Got Him on a Leash

I heard my mother tell a story one day to a group of people in the house about me and my baby sister. The story was about a bad dog on a leash that scared my sister to death. My mother said, "My boy knew something his sister didn't know, that the dog couldn't get to her behind a chain link fence." And I heard her say to others in the room, "My boy said to his screaming sister; 'What's the matter, sister? You scared of that dog? If you are, then don't look at him.' " That was a long time ago and I couldn't believe I said that, as laughter filled the room. We are up in age now and we both found our real daddy who sent his only begotten son to teach us how much he really loves us. As I was studying my Sunday school book, God spoke to me said, "I've got him on a leash. Satan can't do any more than I let him." God placed Job on my mind so I could see Satan going through and forth in the Earth, seeking who he may devour, like a dog on a chain. He makes a lot of noise to scare his victims. He would even whisper in your ears, that he's got you. That you are too sick and you're not going to get well, your finances are too weak, don't pray and trust in the Lord, just lay down and go to sleep, you belong to me. There is no deliverance for you I can see. As I stand and look from the church porch out over God's creation, I smile because I still see my daddy who is the Lord that has the world in his hand. Now I've got the assurance that when trouble comes my way, I can look to the cross and stand on God's word. He spoke over me, You see I'm covered by the blood of Jesus who died on Calvary, but he got up that third day morning after putting a leash on Satan's feet, and declared all power in Heaven and Earth is in His hand.

Put It Away

God said something to me that shook me up. "Put your sword away!" You've got to see me now. After having a good time talking and laughing with my friends, God said, "Put your two-edged sword away, and shut up because you don't see the destruction you're causing."

The tongue can speak life or take it away. When you cut down your brother with unforgiving words, a spiritual death takes place that you just caused to happen, not only to your brother, but to all who heard you and decided and declared in their heart, that's why I don't want their God. Even in the beginning, the spoken tongue caused all of God's creation to pay the price for Adam's choice, which produced a spiritual death to Adam in the Garden. My child, you will be held accountable for the spiritual death you caused by the ill will of your tongue, the sin of omission as well as the sin of commission.

Speak good of your brother. A kind word turns away strife, there is life in the tongue, yet when it goes off to harm, it does just that.

God said love thy brother as thyself.

Resting Place

There is still room in the kingdom, but the problem with us is we wait too long in life to pull over to the side of the road to ask God for direction, or drop to our knees in prayer, so the Lord can meet us there with his arms stretched out to embrace us in His precious love.

Sometimes we act like we are a parked car, waiting on someone else to take us to our journey while we lay back and rest. We are unaware of the friends we keep who are so close to us that they have caused us to be left way out on a limb, so far from home, so far from the Lord.

Let me tell you a story about my journey that began long ago when I was traveling life's highway. There were many weary days and lonely nights that had me seeking to take my life. I can remember many pit stops along the way; I hung out with depression, bathed in lustful thinking, and wrestled with sickness in my flesh. I made many wrong turns before I found a suitable resting place. In a hotel room upon a coffee table lay resting the Word of God for my pleasure. Yet I was too stressed out to read, reaching to shut off the night light (the Holy Bible) that lay on the coffee table. There were many people along my path who tried to guide me to the one who promised me rest. When I think about my Christian journey that led me to many churches that promised me a place which I can set my sight on every day, seeking to reach a place of rest in the Lord, I never dreamed that life would be this hard to stay on the right track. Satan had placed so many pitfalls along my path. God, I need a place of refuge from life's unforgiving test. Not a condo or a duplex house, not even a mansion on the side of a hill, but a place in Jesus. He is the one who God promised us would come to guide me to my place of rest. Matthew 11:28–30. Jesus said, "Come to me, all who are weary and heavy-laden, and I will give you rest."

You Are Covered

It is exciting to hear someone say to you, "You are covered, don't worry about your losses, I'm taking care of your claim, you are in good hands, and I will get back with you in two or three days, but don't relax in thinking it's not going to cost you anything." If it happens once or twice more, that same person would say to you, you are no longer insurable with us due to the number of claims you have filed.

I am one who always tries to fix his own problems and ends up making things worse. But this time, it's good to know you are covered by God's security system, in which the word of God said in the beginning, that the Holy Spirit moves in place and hovered, installing himself over the face of the Earth. When God spoke he performed what God said. I got excited about that, because I can recall a period in my life when I was at a point I was so mad with the world. Why? My house was broken into, and my worldly possessions were taken, no money was left, and I was scared my hurt would cause me to hurt someone else. Now I need a Word. Matthew 6:18–24. I didn't believe in burglar bars because the same bars locked you in while trying to keep the thief out, so I made some wooden bars and bought a shotgun to keep out the intruder. The Holy Spirit spoke up and said, "Will you take a life over worldly possessions?" I didn't answer that, I was still in the flesh, so I went on. Can you believe the thief broke in again and no bars or gun did me any good. The Holy Spirit spoke up again; "Would you take a life over worldly possessions?" I pondered that question and went on, but the Holy Spirit opened my eyes when he said, "You've been covered from the beginning, your life and your soul is covered by God's word," and that's what made all the difference. The real thief wanted to kill, steal, and destroy you. But God wouldn't allow it. He may take your things but he can't touch your life. You are covered.

Do You See What I See?

Do you see what I see? If not, let me take you on a joy ride with me. I wake up in the morning giving thanks to God, for being so good to me. You see, I could have pretended that I woke myself up, but I won't get far down the road thinking like that, so I won't go there.

I need you to get behind my eyes for a moment so you can see what I see. When I shut the car door, I don't see a Chevy or a Ford or any make or model of transportation, but God's glorious chariot, with me in the middle, guarded by God's guardian angel. At this point I'm smiling because I know I'm special. Our celebrities and government leaders have been enjoying specially trained bodyguards, to protect them from seen and unseen dangers when they are out and about. But God dispersed the Holy Ghost to be in me, with my personal guardian angel leading the way, who was trained by God himself, to protect me from seen and unseen dangers not because I am so good but because grace and mercy have got me covered, even from my overdue judgment.

You get excited when you see a celebrity step out of their vehicle, and their security guard push a pathway through a crowd of people to get to their appointed place of business. But when I step out of my chariot I can see my guardian angel pushing back evil spirits, guarding my life from my enemy who is assigned to take me out.

Even if I'm going out to eat, my angel has made reservations to guard me against the cook or the waitress whose life has been disturbed by depressing spirits who don't care who they take out with them.

There were times I was with a crowd of people, and some ungodly things were going on or being said. I can see my guardian angel stepping back out of the way, because they are not allowed to be in the midst of that. Can you see that's when the Holy Ghost begins to rebuke you. I can see my guardian angel waiting on the outside, because he knows God's grace and mercy is guarding me, too.

Even the angels in heaven have said that this is about man who God loves so much.

Can you see, even when I go to my knees to ask God for forgiveness, that He is faithful and just to forgive me and cleanse me from all of my un-righteousness? Yes, I'm covered. I see God's hand all around me.

Talking to the Great Physicians

I have learned now to start looking to hear God's Word for my life, no matter where I am. I ventured out this morning, with my wife, and headed to the hospital with prayer centered on my mind, expecting God to show up and handle our situation, and you know, he did. As my wife went up to surgery, God was there. And as I was seated there in the waiting room, I got a word from God, "You need a physician, too." Calmly, that very moment, I began to check myself. A few aches and pains, but that's normal at my age. Blood pressure is fine, my heart was not racing at any time. "Well, Lord, what do you mean?" Though your body is stable, your spirit is going through cardiac arrest, and if you don't seek me, you are going to die! At a loss for words, as conviction filled my heart, my soul began to ache. Now I know my life has been slipping away from me, due to a lack of the redeeming word not being fed to my mind. I do need to see the great Physician.

In a crowded waiting room I began to seek the Lord. With one Bible, one man in a corner was reading the Word of God. His peace was radiating from his heart because the Word of God was injected into his spirit, which healed his broken heart. IV fluid can try to sustain my flesh, but the Word can restore my health.

Doctor, Lord O Mighty, my great Physician, the healer of all my diseases, the one true and living God, forgive me, Lord, I pray, for I have found out that I am sick, my body weighing a lot and my soul is lighter than a feather. Starving and on life support, held together by your grace and mercy, I seek thee, Lord, now, not later. I need thee, Lord, every hour, my precious Savior.

About the Author

Brother Kerry T. Lee is a local Superintendent and Sunday school teacher of Providence Baptist Church, Birmingham, Alabama. He is a devoted father and husband who graduated from Phillips High in the city of Birmingham. He is a worker who has worked in one place for thirty years, through job changes and company buyouts to job closings.

Brother Lee has been walking with the Lord Jesus Christ from childhood to this present time. The Lord has been his life, with whom he would gladly share what God has done for him, and who has brought him joy, peace, protection and healing for a lifetime. He is the one who calls the Lord "his daddy" in much conversation.